The Playworker's Guide to Playwork

Shelly Newstead

The Buskers Guide to Playwork

ISBN - 1-904792-13-8
© Shelly Newstead 2004

Illustrations © Chris Bennett 2004

Published by Common Threads Publications Ltd.
Upper Market Street
Eastleigh
Hampshire SO50 9FD.
T: 07000 785215
E: info@commonthreads.co.uk

Other titles in The Buskers Guide series include;
The Buskers Guide to Behaviour
The Buskers Guide to Inclusion
The Buskers Guide to Playing Out
The Buskers Guide to Anti-Discriminatory Practice

The text of 'The Buskers Guide...' series can be made available in 14 point font – please contact the publishers by telephoning 07000 785215 or emailing info@commonthreads.co.uk

The Buskers Guide to Playwork

Contents

Introduction

I originally trained as a playworker nearly twenty years ago now, and, let's be honest, I probably wasn't very good at it. We had two days training before being let loose on a school playing field for six weeks on an open-access playscheme with up to 200 children (of dubious ages but we won't go there now!) each day. The training, as far as I can remember, consisted of two basic messages - play is good for children, and before you leave on a trip do please remember to phone the emergency contact first - oh, and have a nice summer. It wasn't bad training - it was actually quite advanced stuff in its time apparently - but it was very different to the sort of stuff that is required now. Back in those days we had no national standards and nobody had even heard of quality assurance. There wasn't even a clear agreement on what playwork was (and some people might say that some things don't change!).

Well, I'm not sure that I knew precisely what we were doing. Despite a 'gut instinct' for play being important, getting a grip on what exactly we were supposed to be doing and how we were supposed to be doing it in order to describe it to myself (never mind others) was a bit tricky. So when I went into playwork training over ten years ago, I probably made a bit of a pigs ear of that too, looking back. Everything was a bit vague and woolly - it was all rather foggy at the time.

But gradually the fog began to clear - and then it was all so obvious that it seemed really strange to me that other people didn't just know this stuff. Why were people still coming on my playwork training courses insisting that whistles were necessary, why were they so sure that getting children to stand in a queue for half an hour to wait to have their faces painted by adults was good playwork practice...? And it didn't matter whereabouts I delivered playwork training, people were telling me the same thing. Nor did it seem to matter how many times I patiently answered the same points in different parts of the UK - people from other parts asked exactly the same questions!

So then I started to get impatient. First of all, I started to feel impatient with the people I was training. Of course, I quickly realised that wasn't fair, because they were only doing what I'd been through - trying to make sense of some very simple and yet complex stuff to put into practice in their daily work with children. So then I got impatient with the people who were already writing playwork books. Every time another one came out, I could be heard whinging, 'It's all very well telling us about health and safety, but could somebody please put in black and white for us why we're not big on displays in playwork so that I don't have to keep going over it every time I do any sort of playwork training!' It felt like it was all starting to wear a bit thin. So finally I got impatient with myself for being impatient (!), and the old adage, 'if you want something doing, do it yourself', came home to me. Whilst it doesn't mean that I'm the best qualified for this particular job, it does mean that I can stop whining about what other people aren't doing!

So there you have it - out of frustration comes creativity, which can't be bad really. My aim in developing the 'Buskers Guide' series was to produce the sort of books that I'd really like everybody to have read before going on any sort of training course, or to be able to give to people to read as part of a training course, so that we can all start with a common understanding of what we're about in the playwork field. That might be egotistical, it might be too much of a tall order, and doubtless there will be people in the playwork field who disagree with the way that I've interpreted some things. But after saying the same things for nearly ten years, I felt that it was about time to say it to more than sixteen people at a time and to save myself some energy!

Two things I need to tell you before we get started. First, all of the practice references and examples, scenes illustrated by the cartoons etc are 'true' - by which I mean that they are things that people have said in training courses, written in assessments of one kind or another, or they have happened to me in my own playwork practice. Thanks to everybody who, over the years, has shared their stories and their experience with me - it's all been part of my own learning and development, and I'm very grateful for that sharing and honesty.

And secondly, what we currently know as the Assumptions and Values of Playwork are being revised at the time of writing, so there is no mention of these (or whatever they turn out to be called next!) in this book. If you don't have a copy of the current ones (whatever they may look like depending on when you are reading this!), you should contact SkillsActive and there are contact details at the back of this book.

And as always at Common Threads, we want and need your feedback to make sure that we're doing what you need us to do. Please send your comments on this book (or anything else for that matter!) to info@commonthreads.co.uk - or by using the other contact methods in the back of this book.

I hope you enjoy the first 'Buskers Guide' - and I look forward to hearing from you!

Shelly Newstead

Chapter 1
Playwork and play

What an odd place to start, I hear you cry! Everybody knows what play is - move on! But hang on a minute - before you skip to Chapter 2, just bear with me for a couple of pages. We could just say 'play is what children do' and leave it at that, but I don't think that's going to help you an awful lot - and one thing I really hate as an author is a bunch of confused readers in the middle of chapter three. So before we go any further, we're just going to get everybody on the same playing field with what people involved in playwork mean by play.

I PLAY THEREFORE I AM

Apologies to Rodin and Descartes.

It seems that the world and his wife (partner/co-habitee/ significant other) has had a go at describing and defining play. Take a look in any standard book of quotations under 'play' and it reads like a roll call of the great and the good. They're all there - poets, philosophers, scholars - all trying to put into words a definitive meaning for what can essentially be described as 'kids mucking about'. But if we take a closer look, we can start to recognise some clear thinking patterns going through all those definitions. It appears that just about everybody believes that play is important and that play is for something. They seem to imply that children play so that something can happen. They say that children learn by playing, become physically healthy by playing, heal emotionally by playing and lots more... In other words, all sorts of good things happen to children because they play.

Which is, of course, good news for children - because you could say that they're naturals at it! Children play all the time and anywhere - they don't need adult permission or provision to do this. If you don't believe me, next time you're in a big supermarket, watch how children use the space as a playground. Wide aisles to run in, freezer doors to slam, people and shop fittings to play hide and seek with, trolleys to provide movement and noise, not to mention the huge number of things in trolleys which all have different textures and colours to explore.... It does make me wonder why adults find shopping boring - perhaps if we all took a couple minutes to play hide and seek in the middle of our local supermarkets we'd feel much better about it!

Anyway, where was I...Ah yes, children are naturals at playing and they can get on with it quite happily on their own and while they're doing it all sorts of good things happen to their physical and emotional development. So far, so good, I think you'd agree. But I'm afraid we're not at Chapter 2 stage yet. Because that's all fine and dandy - until the adults turn up. And adults, being adults, have a habit of interfering - or, as we adults would be more likely to put it, helping. In the case of play, it seems that lots of adults like to lend a helping hand to make sure that play does what it is supposed to.

Now children, time to make sure you get an appropriate amount of social development today!

Now, it could be argued that play does what it does and we adults should just leave well alone. But, let's be fair, some of the interfering can be helpful. The police use games to make children aware of the dangers of criminal activities, teachers use playful methods to help children to get to grips with parts of the curriculum, hospital play specialists use toys to help children to understand what will happen to them during their hospital stay. Play can be a useful way of adults communicating with children, especially in circumstances where children need to understand adult concepts that they find hard to grasp.

What's important for us to get clear in our heads right now is that, as useful as all these adult-led activities are, they are precisely that - adult-led activities. There's nothing wrong with adults using play as a way of communicating with children - far from it, I would even go as far to say that some childrens' lives have probably been saved by adults helping children in this way. But - and here's the really important bit of this chapter - adult-led activities are not what people in playwork mean by play. Playwork uses the word 'play' to mean simply 'what children do if left to their own devices'.

And yes, that's it - it don't get more complicated than that. And at this point on training courses, people usually say - but what about outcomes, what about 'learning through play', what about teaching children right from wrong when they're playing, what about OFSTED, what about me, I'm a playworker, what am I supposed to do? If that's where you're at right now, fear not - we'll get to that later on in this book. For now I need you to hang on to the fact that, in playwork terminology, play is essentially for and by children and all those other things are adult stuff which have no place in playwork. In fact many people in playwork would argue that the more adults get involved in children's play, the less children play, and so all the informal learning and development that would naturally happen anyway gets lost as a result of the adult involvement. Which sorts of defeats the object, I guess!

Before we go any further, let's just make sure we're all happy with some of the terminology we're going to use for the rest of the book.

Play and Activities

In playwork terminology, 'play' and 'activities' are different beasties.

'Activities' can loosely be defined in playwork terms as 'things for children to do'. Activities generally;

❖ Need specific or specialist equipment
❖ Have fixed boundaries or rules
❖ Are adult-led, directed or supervised
❖ Result in an end product

❖ Have a specific way of achieving the end product. In order to 'do' activities, children have to understand the instructions, follow the rules that go with that particular activity and carry out actions in a certain way in order to be involved in the activity.

Examples of activities could be;

❖ Making something from wood using woodwork tools
❖ Candle making
❖ Putting on a play
❖ Board games
❖ Organised sports and team games.

Once again, there's nothing wrong with 'activities', as long as we recognise them as activities and don't confuse them with 'play'. Activities can offer children new experiences which they do not have access to elsewhere and they can also be useful in helping children to combat boredom or to develop specific skills. And, if adults get it right, activities can also result in children playing - but let's not jump ahead, we'll deal with that one in Chapter 4. For now, let's stick to what we've got so far - 'play' and 'activities' are different, and while children can play easily without activities being organised for them, they'll find it more difficult to play if activities are organised for them and that's the only thing that's on offer.

'Play opportunities'

Before we go on, we'll just pause here for a moment to deal with the term 'play opportunities'. This phrase has crept into playwork vocabulary in recent years and it's pretty confusing - sometimes it seems to mean 'activity', and sometimes I don't think that anybody knows what it does mean! As far as I can see, pretty much everything is a 'play opportunity' for a child - the large rocks on the beach that can be dropped onto crabs' heads, those big vertical freezer doors in the supermarket that make a satisfying 'plop' noise when you slam them hard, a table with a cloth over it which can become many different places to hide.

So let's keep it simple - if it's child-led it's play, if it's adult-led it's activities. And just about the whole world is a 'play opportunity' to a child, so that phrase is now officially useless! (You heard it here first....!)

Playwork and play

So, I hope by now that we're all on the same playing field when it comes to playwork and play. When we talk about play in playwork terms, we don't mean adults telling children how to spend their free time or even, however well-intentioned we might be, organising activities to help along children's development. We mean children deciding for themselves what they are going to do, how they are going to do it, when they are going to do it and who they are going to do it with.

So if I could place a mental image in your head right now to get us from Chapter 1 to Chapter 2, it would be this...While we're standing on our playing field, we have not got whistles around our necks, nor nice straight lines of children standing quietly waiting to be told what to do next. Instead we're standing around looking a bit nonplussed with our hands in our pockets whilst the kids are doing whatever it is they are doing all over the field.

And ok, I lied about the couple of pages - but it was worth it, wasn't it?! Now on to Chapter 2 to look at what playwork is about....

Chapter 2
What is Playwork?

So now we're happy with the word 'play' in the context of playwork, we can get on with looking at the word playwork itself. 'Playwork' is a word that is currently used in all sorts of different ways. Before we can understand what playwork is all about, we need to get to grips with the two main different ways that the word is used. These can be summed up like this;

❖ 'Playwork' is a methodology: that is, a distinct way of working with children
❖ 'Playwork' can be a service, delivered by adults for children, either through people, places or a combination of both.

Playwork - the methodology

'Playwork' is a way of working with children which enables children to play in the way that they want - and some would argue, need - to play. There is no adult-led 'agenda' when it comes to playwork - no attempt to try to 'make' things happen when children play, or to get children to play in certain ways. The content and the form of play is therefore left up to the children and the value of that play is judged by the children themselves. There are no goals to achieve nor outcomes to meet, neither by children nor adults.

So, if playwork is 'simply' about children playing, why do adults need to come into the picture at all? As we said in Chapter 1, it could be argued that adults should just leave play to do what it does anyway, as well-intentioned adults can sometimes prevent children from playing rather than helping them. But there are several reasons why children end up playing under the supervision of adults;

❖ Children suffer a lack of open space in which to play on their own, because of lack of gardens, no school playing fields, limited access to public space and so on
❖ Adult and childrens' fears about playing unsupervised in public spaces because of perceived and real threats to safety, such as 'stranger danger', traffic, street crime etc
❖ Some children have limited access to stimulating play environments because of lack of resources in their families
❖ Many children now attend supervised provision as a result of adult needs for time, childcare, respite etc.

For all of those reasons and others, more and more children now find themselves regularly making use of supervised provision - in some cases through their own choice, or because they are told they have to. So, if more and more children need supervised provision, there has to be an increase in the number of adults doing the supervising. Many more adults are therefore finding themselves gaining access to a part of children's culture that has not traditionally been paid an awful lot of attention by adults.

Playwork is of course not a new thing. It has existed for decades in a variety of contexts to safeguard the play needs of children. But in today's world, we can say that the playwork methodology is an adult response to children being less likely to have opportunities to play, both on their own and on their own terms.

To put it another way, if all adults who are responsible for supervising children only allow children to do what the adults want, then children will have less and less opportunity to play - which, as we've said already, cannot be a good thing. Playwork is therefore a way of working with children which enables children to play both as a result of, and despite, adult presence.

So that's why playwork the methodology exists - to ensure that children can still have the opportunity to play, even if they are spending the majority of time under the beady eye of some adult somewhere. But what is this methodology - how can we describe what it is? Well, it's quite simple really...*playwork is the art and science of facilitating children's play.*

Why an art? Because in order to facilitate play, it is necessary to have several skills, many of which rely heavily on 'gut instinct' and an acute awareness of ourselves and of others. Playwork requires the knack of understanding children's play needs and responding appropriately to them.

Now then, am I respondin in an appropriat way?

Why a science?
Because the playwork methodology is based on sound theory from playwork practitioners and related play disciplines.

And what about facilitation? Facilitators are people who make things easier for others. People who use the playwork methodology make it easier for children to play, and we'll see how this works in practice in the next couple of chapters.

So lots of adults who work with children for specific purposes can also use playwork as a methodology in their work. For example, playwork can be used as a way of working with children in schemes to make visiting easier in prison, or in a childcare service for parents such as an after school care club, or in schools by adults during break times.

Whoever is doing it, the key to using playwork as a methodology is to be clear that that is what the adults are doing. By using playwork they are helping children to play for play's sake, not for any other purpose or agenda. They may also have to use different methods of working with children to achieve other parts of their work, such as social and moral education for example, as the playwork methodology will not give them this opportunity.

In order to 'do playwork', adults must do three things;

1. Provide an environment fit for play
2. Understand how and when to get involved in children's play
3. Use reflective practice to inform their playwork practice.

Don't worry, you're not on your own from here on in - the rest of this book will describe what this means and how to put it into practice. But before we get to that bit, we just need to finish this chapter first!

Playwork - the service

The other use of the word 'playwork' is to describe a service put on for children by adults who only use the playwork methodology. This 'service' could look like a person (a playworker) or a place. It would of course be impossible to have a place where playwork happened without any playworkers there, although play would take place anyway if children were there!

However, it is possible to have playworkers who do not have a fixed space in which to offer a playwork service. There are many playworkers who pack up some kit in a wheelbarrow (or something that looks like a wheelbarrow at least!) and turn up on a piece of open ground and wait for the children to come to them.

Playwork services include;

* ❖ Adventure playgrounds
* ❖ Open access playschemes
* ❖ Playbuses
* ❖ 'Play in the park'/park ranger schemes.

It is of course the case that these settings may also serve different purposes and agendas in some of their work. Play sessions on playbuses, for example, can be used as a focus for building community projects, adventure playgrounds may operate specific initiatives for children with special needs for respite purposes, and so on. However, the people working at these type of projects will usually be playwork trained first and foremost, whilst some may also have developed other skills relevant to their particular service.

Playwork - the profession

So, I hear you wondering, that's it then, is it? Playwork is about helping children to play and you can do that in a park or in an adventure playground and you can get paid for it - what a doss! You may, however, not be surprised to hear that I'm about to contradict you if that's where you're at right now! Contrary to the old adage 'anyone can work with children', not everybody can be a playworker and some adults find that the playwork methodology puts them into uncomfortable places to be. In the realm of the playing child, reality can often look - and feel - very different. Some adults can feel uncomfortable with this different take on reality and some adults even find it disturbing.

When children are playing in the 'playwork' sense of the word, children play a range of real-life and pretend situations, they experiment with language and boundaries, they take risks. Through doing so they experience the whole range of emotions - from fear to happiness, anger to exhilaration.

The very nature of playwork means that adults are going to be around when children access the range of play experiences and the emotions that go with them. Children will play in the way that they choose at the time when they feel most comfortable, not when the adult feels comfortable. Children can become very absorbed in their play, and this can also be disconcerting for some adults, particularly if the subject of their playing is not one that we would consider to be 'nice'.
The problem is, that if adults are uncomfortable about children's play, we can then go into what I describe as 'control and contain' mode - in other words, we become prescriptive about what and how children play. And then we are stop 'playworking' - making it easier for the child to play. Instead we make it harder, by projecting our fears onto children and trying to make the world a neat and tidy place, both for them and for us.

If we step back for a moment, we know that children need to be able to deal with the world as it is, not how we would like it to be, both now and in the future. Play is a perfectly normal way of children being able to do this. In other words, they need to play - however bad that might make some of us adults feel. Some adults cannot use the playwork methodology when working with children as it is just too uncomfortable for them to do so, and so they use their skills to work with children in different ways instead, which is as it should be.

It is also important in playwork terms to be able to separate out our playwork role from other roles we may fulfil in childrens' lives. For example, those of you working in playwork who are also parents may find that you have to apply different standards in the playwork role to those you would live by at home. Adults who work with children across a range of different roles (for example, teaching in term times and playworking in the summer holidays) often have to 'get their playwork head on' and move mentally from the way they work with children in school to the way that the

playwork methodology requires them to work with children. This can be difficult for adults to achieve, but very important so that the children's opportunity to play without adult agendas is protected.

Playwork - the movie

Sorry, only kidding - just checking you're still with me - that last bit got a bit heavy!

So, to sum it all up so far then....playwork is a methodology, a distinct way of working with children, and it can be offered as part of adult's wider roles in working with children or as a 'stand alone' service. Playwork is not the same as;

❖ Teaching
❖ Youthwork
❖ Sports leadership
❖ Informal education
❖ Parenting

...although it is true to say that any adults working within those areas could use playwork as part of their role.

Playwork is not concerned with anybody else's needs except for those of children, and more specifically, the play needs of the children. For example, whilst some adults may use the playwork methodology in childcare settings, if it is the parents' concerns which take priority over the children's play needs (for example, banning 'messy play' over parental concerns about clothes), then the adults working in that setting cannot be said to be playworking.

Playwork is not anarchy or chaos, a lawless state where 'anything goes'. Playwork only exists because adults put themselves in spaces where children play. As such, those adults have clearly defined legal responsibilities and playworkers and other adults who use the playwork methodology must be aware of those requirements and know how to put them into place in the context of playwork.

In the next three chapters we're going to take a look at the three things we said that adults need to do in order to 'do playwork', starting with the playwork environment.

Chapter 3
Playwork Places

If playwork is the art and science of facilitating play, then it has to happen somewhere, right? We've already agreed (I hope!) in the previous chapters that children can play at any time and anywhere, but we also need to look at what helps children to play - because if our role is to make it easier for children to play, then we should be doing some thinking about what they need!

Play Value

...or, as I also call it, the cardboard box theory. What do children play with most of all when they receive a present - the battery-powered gizmo that flashes lights, says 'hello' and fires a laser gun, or the cardboard box that it came in? Yes, I know that's an easy one, but I do like to go gently on you at the start of a chapter! Of course it's the box - and why? Because it has more play value.

In other words, a child can usually play more with - or, *can get more play out of* - a cardboard box than they can from whatever's inside it. Cardboard boxes have endless possibilities - they can become anything that's in the child's imagination, whilst your battery-powered gizmos look like something and were obviously intended to be used in a certain way. Now of course children can and do use the gizmos in different ways for their play - but it's more difficult to do this, and children will play longer with something that has higher play value, like a cardboard box.

Children in supervised play places need 'stuff' around them that has high play value. (They also need to be allowed to use this 'stuff' in whatever way they fancy, otherwise there's no point in it having loads of play value - but we'll get to that in the next chapter!) Children who are not in supervised play spaces are able to choose from a whole load of different things to play with, and therefore select the things that have more interest for them - that it, the stuff with more play value. So any place where playwork is going to take place, be that a playbus, a prison or an adventure playground, has to make sure that equipment, resources and toys it offers to children have high play value.

Just what sort of things are we talking about here? Well, get a load of things together around you from wherever you are sitting and put them in front of you. Then let your imagination go wild and see how much play you can get out of each thing individually. It's a bit hard for me to envisage what you're doing right now (for which maybe I should be grateful!), but my guess would be that if you've taken off your sock and gathered together a mug and a pen, you are going to be having more fun with the sock and perhaps nearly as much fun with the pen. The mug I find a little more challenging! (Some of you might have had a go at playing with all three together - that's cheating, 'cos that's in the next chapter!)

So that's play value - how much play can you get out of something. If we then think about children's toys, we can soon see why LEGO® is the most successful toy of all time - endless things to do with those bricks. Well, there is if we don't restrict children to those shapes that somebody else has made - that's why we throw away those glossy leaflets that come with any sort of construction kits in playwork, by the way! In playwork we also respect the child's decision about the play value of toys and equipment - it's not for the adults to decide whether toys are 'age appropriate' or can be played with only by certain children (girls/boys), for example. If a child is playing with something, it's because they think it is worth playing with - that's good enough for us!

And, of course, playwork is not just about providing toys for children to play with. As we know from the cardboard box theory, children can play with anything, and there is heaps of play value in paper, pasta, sticks, stones, bits of cloth and material, etc etc. Not forgetting, of course, my all-time favourite - string. Even if some playwork places don't have such easy access to the outdoors, it is easy enough to offer trips to children so that they can play in the outdoors, and, in the meantime, bring some of the outdoors in. Heaps of earth on plastic sheeting might not be as high play value as digging holes outside, but it's got a darn sight more play value than colouring sheets! So anywhere that's offering playwork to children has to have lots and lots of this sort of stuff available to children at all times.

Remember the discussion we had in Chapter 1 about activities? Activities, by their very nature, limit children in how they go about using the equipment. Playwork says, 'Here's some stuff, whad'ya reckon?' (And, of course, the adults have thought in advance about the play value which the 'stuff' offers to the children.) Again, it's worth recognising that some adults find that a bit disconcerting - for some of us it's been a long time since we took off one of our socks and played with it!

Play space

Whilst we're on the subject of activities, we'll just spend some time here thinking about the physical space that needs to be available for playworking. To put it in a nutshell, activity schemes have activities (usually on tables) in certain places and designated spaces for things to happen (for example, a home corner from which certain items must not be moved in case they stray into the 'messy play' area). This is fine and fit for purpose, but it's different to a space which offers playwork, which simply says to children, 'This is your space, it's got some stuff in it, now over to you to work out how to use it - or not, if you've got better ideas.'

Playwork spaces also offer space - I know that sounds silly, but it's quite important, honest! When children are playing, they need space - space to hop on one foot for no particular reason, space to build dens, space to play fight, space to hang out and tell jokes with their mates - and they can't do this if every square inch is designated by adults for a particular purpose. So instead of succumbing to that adult tendency to 'fill every gap and make it look as if we're doing something here', adults creating playwork places make sure that there is room for children to play, as well as stuff for them to play with. After all, if children want to cover half the floor with dozens of bits of paper (don't ask me why, it's play, it doesn't matter why!), then they need the floor space to do it!

'Space' in playwork terms is not only physical, it also mental space that playworking offers children. Instead of saying, 'Here's some cardboard boxes, today we're going

to make a robot', playwork simply says, 'Here's some cardboard boxes - use them or ignore them, whatever you feel like!' I've seen many adults getting really upset because the children didn't appear to think that the adults' ideas were the best when it came to what to do with the 'stuff'. But if they had been playworking, those adults would have simply been interested in what the children were doing with the stuff - or even what they weren't doing...Sorry, I'm digressing again into Chapter 4!

Play people

As well as 'stuff' and space, children also sometimes need other people to play with. Sometimes they don't, and are perfectly happy to play on their own - but playwork places have people available if a child decides that they want to play with somebody else. So a playwork place makes sure that children and adults are free to play. Adults don't divide children into groups (or teams for that matter, children can do that) according to age, ability or any other artificially-adult-created concept, neither do we set times for things certain things or varieties of play to happen. Nor do we give adults, who should be available to facilitate play if needed, jobs to do which take them off elsewhere. Somebody in the kitchen all session, somebody staffing the tuckshop, somebody up a ladder putting up a display and somebody cleaning the toilets leaves me wondering - who's playing with the kids if they want us to?! Or

even, who's observing how the children are playing and what they are playing with to make sure that they have got enough/the right sort of/good play value 'stuff'?

To put it another way, the more time adults spend organising children and other adults to 'do things', the less playmates the children will have available to them. And the point of playwork is - yep, that's right, it's about play, so let's make sure there are lots of play people available in our playwork places.

Of course, some places which offer playwork also offer food, so some people do need to be in the kitchen, and of course toilets need cleaning wherever children are! So somebody's got to do that - but we need to make sure that it's not at the expense of children's play.

Providing a playwork place

Just to sum up then - a playwork place has got three vital ingredients; 'stuff' with high play value, space for children to play and people (both children and adults) who are available for play if needed. And just in case you're thinking at this stage - 'how much room do we need?', let's just think about this logically. Even with the smallest of floor spaces, adults can choose whether to put in that space some colouring books and pencils, a craft activity and a board game (all relatively low play value), or some string, some junk and glue and various sizes and textures of material (vastly more play value). Those adults can also decide how to present that equipment - all over our tiny playwork place so it looks like there's no room for anything else to happen, or all together at one end so there appears to be tons of room to play with the stuff in or do whatever else the children feel like in that space? And then the adults can decide how they're going to offer the play space to children - 'here's the string, junk, glue and material and today we're going to make a robot!' or 'here's the string, junk, glue and material and some space.' Play places then are not limited by their physical size, they are only limited by how adults offer them. Which brings us nicely to Chapter 4 at last!

Chapter 3.5
Playwork Planning

Sorry, I fibbed slightly at the end of the last chapter - we just need to do this bit first. Because at this point in training courses, adults inevitably metaphorically roll up their sleeves and say, 'Right, we got the space sorted out, now what do we do?' And I say, 'Not a lot, you've done the hard bit now.' And people start to look a bit worried... 'But we have to do something - what about planning, we need to do some planning, or we're not going to know what to do!' And I say, 'Bit tricky that.' And then there's a bit of a silence whilst the

This wasn't part of our plan.

group has a think about that one - and then one by one they start to grin at me.

Because the point is, of course, how can we plan play? Only children can do that. And actually, most of the time in my experience they don't, because play is generally spontaneous and 'of and in the moment.'

Some of us will have had the fascinating experience of observing children 'getting ready to play' - setting up a shop scenario, for example. And the reason that this is fascinating for me is that they are actually playing whilst they are doing the 'setting up'. In fact, by the time they are 'ready to start', most or all of them have lost interest, because they've already 'rehearsed' playing shop and, in doing so, they've finished with that piece of play and so move on to play something else.

So adults can't plan play because play is always under the control of the children. And children are unlikely to plan play because, by its very nature, they can't really. And yet this term 'planning' has crept into playwork terminology and has somehow come to mean 'timetables of things to do with children', or 'timetables of things for children to do.' Which inevitably turn out to look like activities - which as we've already said elsewhere, is fine if adults want to run activity schemes. But if they intended to offer playwork, then timetables of activities are not going to do it, I'm afraid.

And yes, there is at the time of writing, legislation around which tells some of us adults offering playwork to do some planning in the context of facilitating children's play. But that is pretty much all it says - it doesn't tell us what to plan or how to do it - and it certainly doesn't require us draw up timetables.

But if we don't do timetables, what do we do? Well, it's actually much easier than drawing up timetables in fact. All we have to do in playwork (to show that we don't just turn up, drink tea and watch kids play each session), is show how we think about and prepare the environment for children to play in. And basically this is the stuff we did in Chapter 3 - we make judgements about the play value, we make decisions the use of space, we work out how to make people available for play. We may also choose a particular play theory on which to base our work (this particular bit is beyond the scope of a 'Buskers Guide' I'm afraid, but there's lots in the bibliography to help with this one!).

And we think about all these things on a regular basis and we take action according to what we think should happen next. Now if that's not planning in playwork terms, I don't know what is. Playworkers are interested in children's responses to the play environment and react to that if necessary - to try to 'plan' that is to put the cart before the horse!

All we need to do then, is to review all those things on a regular basis (daily, weekly, monthly possibly, according to how you're playworking) and write it all down (yes, I know it's a drag but it's worth it to get rid of those timetables, trust me!). Then keep the pieces of paper to show to whoever really wants to know about your planning. (Some experienced playworkers, by the way, have told me that they do the timetable thing 'just to keep them happy' but then ignore the timetables and just get on with facilitating play instead. Sound principle, but if we got it across to 'them' - whoever 'they' might be! - what we're doing in the first place, then we wouldn't have to put so much wasted effort into drawing up paperwork that we are just going to ignore.)

What we really have to remember is that plans are for adults, not for children. We do plans in playwork to make sure that we are meeting children's play needs as best we can - not so that what children do in the play space fits our pieces of paper. Easy, right? Good - now we can get on with the really interesting stuff...

Chapter 4
Adults and play

In Chapter 3 we looked at what adults can provide to facilitate play. It would be great if it was that easy - then we could just wander off to leave the kids to do what they do! But, as we said in Chapter 1, playwork exists because adults find themselves having to be present in children's play environments. So as well as making sure that the space is right for children to play, we also have to make sure that the way we act within this space is also geared up to facilitate play. This chapter then is about playwork skills - what adults need to do - or not do in some cases! - to facilitate play.

Offering choice

It sounds easy enough, doesn't it? Playworking means offering choices to children in how they play. They've got loads of stuff, they've got the space, they've got the people - so all they need now is for adults to stand back and let them get on with it. And that's what we mean in playwork terms by 'choice'. Choice in playwork does not mean, 'Would you like to play rounders or cricket - or if you don't want to do either of those, there's drawing instead over there.' Neither does it mean that children are split into groups and given the choice of whether they do crafts in the morning or the afternoon. These are options for children, fair enough, but it's not choice as we know it (Jim)! Playwork is about offering children the choice of when and how they play, who and what they play with - or not as the case maybe. (Ask children what they like about their playwork places best and very often the answer will be 'Having a chat with my mates.' Not to be actively engaged in play is also a good choice for children - apart from anything else, playing all the time can be quite exhausting!)

Respecting children's choices

One of the consequences of offering children the choice of how they play is that adults then have to respect the choices that children make. This is all very well in theory, but in practice how do you feel about children playing 'wars' and making guns to 'kill' each other with? And what about children who always want to 'roughhouse' or tickle each other? As we said in Chapter 2, some sorts of children's play make some adults uncomfortable. But the thing is, we're there to make it easier for children to play - in all its forms, not just the bits that we think are 'acceptable'. The bottom line has to be that, if it's play, it's ok - there is no such thing as 'good play' and 'bad play', it's just play. We adults must not stigmatise certain children who play in a certain way. Instead we need to take some adult responsibility and deal with why certain sorts of play make us feel uncomfortable, rather than pass on our hang-ups onto children who are after all, just doing what comes naturally.

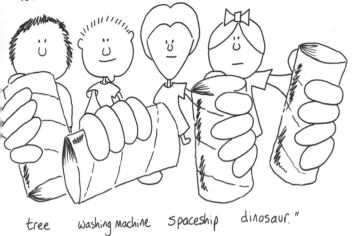

"It's a...

tree   washing machine   spaceship   dinosaur."

One of the other ways that adults respect children's choices in playwork is by not restricting children's use of materials. We talked about play value in Chapter 3 - well, a paper plate can have a thousand and one play uses to a child - it doesn't have to be limited to the craft activity that adults plan. So adults using playwork do not, for example, tell children that they can only use the paper plates on the craft table. In Chapter 1 we said that activities could lead to play - but only if children are allowed to use the materials for the activity in the way that they choose. So the paper plate, for example, could increase in play value if the children end up playing 'flying saucers' with it across the room. If they are told to only use it for a craft, then the play value decreases lots.

Children also combine unlikely items to increase their play value. Or, to put it another way, think back to Chapter 3 when I asked you to decide on the play value of some items around you. Now decide how much more play value you would get out of playing with your pen, sock and mug at the same time. All of a sudden that mug has many more play uses, right?! And so it is when children play - which is why adults using playwork respect children's choices about what they play with and how they play with it. After all, as we said in Chapter 3, there is no point in stuff having high play value if we don't let children make full use of it!

Observation skills

To those who are not in the know, it might look like adults who are playworking are standing around being

idle for quite a lot of the time. But we know different. They are actually using their observation skills of course - one of the most important skills when it comes to facilitating play.

Just what are they observing? Well, in terms of the children's play, they are watching to see if children want them to play with them - this may be very subtlety done with just a glance or a smile from a child, so adults need to be quite good at observation for this reason alone. They are also observing how children use resources, so that they can reflect on whether further or different sorts of resources are needed.
Adults also observe so that they can pick up when children can be offered support - perhaps they're trying to climb a tree and can't quite get it right, at which point an adult might offer help. Adults also need observation skills to pick up the clues about when to leave children to it because they can play perfectly well without any adult interference.

Adults who are playworking need the information from their observations to make judgements on how to make it easier for children to play. This could mean using this information to join in or to leave well alone!

Asking questions and making suggestions

Sometimes, as a result of our observations, we may decide that children need some sort of help, either to keep their playing going or to start it off again in a different form. This form of help is offered as suggestions or ideas, rather than telling the child how to do something. Adults are sometimes all too quick to give children answers so that children can 'get it right'. What we're not so good at remembering sometimes is that, in play, there really isn't a right or a wrong answer, and as it's the child's play and not ours, the final decision should always be the child's.

So if a child complains that they have run out of purple paint and they need some more, the playwork response is not, 'Well, I'll mix together some blue and some red for you', it's 'Ok, so what happens next?' It maybe that the child really does want to use more purple paint, in which case mixing could be the next suggestion, but it might be that the question sparks off another playful train of thought for the child. 'Well, I don't know, but maybe I could leave it white 'cos that's the bit where the ghosts live anyway..' Enter an opportunity for a ghost story perhaps?

In the same vein, if a child asks an adult to draw a camel for them, the playwork response is never, 'Oh yes, I'm very good at drawing', whilst conjuring up a perfect

image of a dromedary to proudly present to the child. Instead, we ask the child a question to spark off the play process, 'A camel, eh? How many humps has it got? You draw one, I'll draw the other...does our camel have a name...?' and so on, until you have both engaged in a playful process to create a camel. It might not look like your average camel, but we're facilitating play, so that is really not the point!

Being playful

I suppose this is really obvious, but it's worth saying anyway...Adults who are facilitating play need to be playful themselves. This is not the same as being irresponsible, or forgetting that we are adults, but sometimes children look for playful responses in adults to further develop their play and we need to help them along by being playful.

For example, a child comes into the play space crawling on all fours yapping, 'I'm Fluffy the dog, woof woof!', the playwork response is not, 'Get up off that filfthy floor Johnny, you'll ruin your trousers'! But rather something like, 'Hello Fluffy! Go fetch the ball and I'll throw it for you - good boy Fluffy!' This type of response will help the child to play longer - the first response will just make him feel daft, which is not a good thing!

Playworking requires that adults role model playing for children - no matter how silly that may make us feel! By playing ourselves we send out the message to children that playing is a good thing and there aren't really any rights or wrongs when playing.

Being playful also means that we need to be cheerful - even if we don't really feel like it - both in ourselves and with individual children. Neither children nor adults can play in an atmosphere of gloom and high dudgeon!

Being sensitive to children's playful states

Again, the observation skills come in really handy here. Children get absorbed in their play, both when they're playing alone or in groups. Having an adult yell, 'Right, stop what you're doing right now, it's time to go home!' can jolt

children out of their playful states very suddenly. We know ourselves that if somebody interrupts us without warning when we are concentrating hard on something, then we can feel really disorientated and a bit put out. This can have the same effect on children when they are playing, because the play process absorbs them so deeply. So it is important in playwork to be sensitive to children's playful states, and to make sure that these are protected as far as possible.

If other things have to happen in the play space, such as food for example, then it doesn't actually have to happen at the same time on the dot every day just because it always has. It is more important to observe where children are at in their play and to decide when (or even whether) it is appropriate to interrupt them, in the light of their play needs. This is also important to bear in mind when it comes to 'home time' - if children are absorbed in their play they need a gentle countdown to make them aware that their time for playing is coming to an end.

During play, children decide when they move in and out of a playful state. Adults need to respect that when children want to move on to another piece of play, that is what they should be able to do. So adults who are playworking do not ask children to 'finish things off' before they start on a different piece of play - if it's 'finished' for them it's finished for us!

And last, but definitely not least...

Of course, this is just what we need to do to offer children the 'play' part of playworking. There's all the other side of playwork for adults to take on board too, things which this book doesn't cover but there are plenty of resources listed in the bibliography that do. I am of course talking about things like risk assessment, health and safety issues, legal requirements around things like adult/child ratios and so on, all of which have an impact on playwork and how it is offered to children. What we have to remember, though, is that we interpret and apply legislation and so on within the context of 'doing playwork', not the other way round. It is definitely beyond the scope of this book to go into any more detail on this here, but Chapter 3.5 gives some handy hints on where to start!

Chapter 5
Are we doing it right?

Playworking is a funny thing really. Not in the 'funny ha-ha' sense (although you could say that there should be quite a bit of that if we're doing it right!), but in the sense that, most of the time and on a day-to-day level, it has to be down to our own personal judgement as to whether we're doing what we're supposed to. It would be really nice to be able to tell you at this stage of the book that, as long as you're doing everything the previous chapters tell you, you'll get it right every time.

But, of course, life is never that simple - especially when we work with people, and especially when some of those people are children. People in general (and, it could be said, children in particular!) do not come with a full set of instructions, which is a shame in one way, but on the other hand I guess it makes life much more interesting! Instead, playwork has the theories and models to get us off the starting blocks and inform us about the general direction in which to head. But we have to admit that they're not a lot of use for letting us know if we get to the right finishing post, or whether we've joined a different race entirely along the way. (This has often happened to me whilst playworking by the way - it's not necessarily a bad thing, but you do have to be able to see clearly behind you to be able to understand how you got there!)

It's true, of course, that most of us will have managers, assessors, mentors, supervisors and other people who can give us feedback on our playwork practice. But even they are not there all the time, observing our every move. So we need to develop our way of thinking about what we're doing and what we've done in order to make sure that we are on the right track - even if it is a different one to the one we started off on! And this type of thinking is called reflective practice.

Reflective practice can be described as a form of self-evaluation. If we're aware of what we're doing and how we're doing it, we can then use that information to;

❖ Check that we're doing playwork when we mean to do playwork and are not veering off into other ways of working with children

❖ Make sure that we're applying playwork methodology rather than using our personal experiences and values to interact with children

❖ Solve problems by applying knowledge or approaches from similar situations in the past

❖ Save ourselves time and energy looking for 'the answer' when it might be that none exists because it's actually an 'approach' we need instead

❖ Use playwork models and theories to inform and develop our practice.

To use reflective practice effectively, there are several things that we adults need to accept about ourselves. First and foremost, we need to accept that we are not perfect. If we were perfect, if we knew what to say or do all the time and got it right every time, then we wouldn't need to use reflective practice. And let's face it, it would be a major miracle if that were the case. So we have to be honest with ourselves and accept that we can and do get things wrong from time to time, or at least that some of the things we have done could have been done better. We also need to accept that our personal practice will - and should - change as a result of reflective practice. Or in other words, we shouldn't be afraid to admit (to ourselves and others) that we've done things differently in the past and that's a positive thing - and who knows, we'll probably do them differently again in the future!

Finally, we need to accept that changes and development are all part of the reflective practice process and not to take this personally. Developing our practice doesn't mean that we are bad at playworking, it means that we take our responsibilities as adults in childrens' play environments seriously. And that can only be a good thing! Do you remember when I said in Chapter 2 that not all adults are good at playwork? Well, hopefully now you can see another reason why - some adults want and need to be - and be seen to be - 'in the right' and 'in control' all the time. This makes it very hard for them to develop reflective practice skills, as part of this process is owning up to the need to do things differently sometimes. Adults who can't do this find it very hard to have children moving the goalposts around them all of the time - and let's face it, what else should we expect when working in children's play?!

5 stage reflective practice model

Ok, now we know what it's for and why it's important, we need to put some shape to how we actually do reflective practice. Or, to put it another way, if any of you are now thinking that reflective practice is tantamount to crystal ball - or, at best, navel - gazing, then this is the bit where we get serious!

We can break down the reflective practice process into five parts, which are;

1. **Intention**
2. **Experience**

3. **Interaction**
4. **Outcome**
5. **Development**

Reflective practice is a structured process which needs a bit of time and thought to get it to be almost 'second nature' when playworking. Each part of the process serves a very particular purpose...

1. **Intention**
First of all, we need to ask ourselves what was it that we set out to do. Maybe it was to act in line with a particular model or theory - if so, which one and how did we set about achieving what we felt we should?

2. **Experience**
Next we need to recall what actually happened - almost put together a mini-story of how the whole thing took place.

3. **Interaction**
Then we need to look more closely at our part in the whole event - what did we say, what did we feel, what were we thinking and so on. This is where the honesty bit comes in, as we need to make sure that we are remembering what actually happened, not what we think should have happened instead!

4. **Outcome**

Now we need to ask how what we intended to happen at the start actually turned out. Did what we want to take place actually happen, or did things that we said or did (or even thought and felt!) get in the way and prevent what we intended from actually taking place? Again, honesty is really important here!

5. **Development**

So, what have we learnt? Did we achieve what we originally set out to do? If so, what was it that we said/did/thought/felt that helped that to happen? If the outcome wasn't what we'd hoped - why not, and what made it happen differently? Is there anything we can notice for next time to help us to get to where we need to be?

It's worth mentioning here that there are actually two types of reflective practice using that model...

Continuous reflective practice - this is a bit like having a sound-track of what you're doing and how you're doing it in your head all the time. This is fairly advanced playworking and takes a fair bit of practice (and some getting used to if I'm honest!), but it's really useful once you've got the hang of it as it can help us to improve our playworking literally as we're doing it.

Specific reflective practice - this is the more 'traditional-after-the-event' sort of reflection where we reflect on an event or interaction some time away from when it actually took place. One of the advantages of this type of reflective practice is that it can be done with other people, who could see things differently to you!

Reflective practice then is a really important part of playworking. No two children are the same, no two days are ever the same, and so very often there is no absolutely clear-cut answer for the way that we need to act when facilitating play. It's up to us to make sure that we're using the principles and models that we're given in playwork to guide the way we act and think when playworking. Reflective practice is the thing that helps us to keep an eye on whether we're doing this - or if not, what we're going to do about it!

And finally...

It seems that there are always those 'frequently asked questions' that people who are getting their head around playwork need answering. So here they are - I hope they tie up any loose ends for you too!

'I've heard the phrase 'process not product' used - what does this actually mean?'

It's about the fact that in playwork, we're not interested in outcomes or 'end products'. Children in playwork places start and finish their play whenever it suits them,

"Picture orders... yes, at the moment we have sheep made with cotton wool or ducks decorated with scrunched up tissue paper — yes, they are all suitable for fridge doors. "

not when something has been completed to the adult's satisfaction. So playwork focuses on the process of playing, rather than the need to get something out of it.

'Should we not put up displays of the children's artwork then?'

In short - no! If the children want to put their stuff up on the walls - great. But they must be allowed to do that as a part of their play process, not because they want to please an adult. Apart from the fact that if adults are busying themselves with putting up displays they are not available to observe and play, we can easily stray into all sorts of murky areas around adult judgements of children's creativity. Displays are done in other forms of work with children and for good reason, but those good reasons do not fit with the playwork methodology.

'How are we supposed to make sure that children are safe if they're all doing different things at different times?'

Well, first of all you will be observing children playing and so can pick up any safety issues as and when you need to. And most importantly, adults using playwork will make risk assessments before, during and after the play sessions to ensure appropriate safety for the children they are working with.

'Somebody told me that we can't let children play with toilet rolls or egg boxes?'

Ah yes, I'm really glad you brought that one up! This is actually one of what I call a 'playwork old wives tale' (with a courteous nod in the direction of old wives!). As far as I understand it, it is supposed to be in case children catch germs of some description. But this is not actually carved in tablets of stone, neither is it written in any legislation that I can find! Anything that children play with has to be risk-assessed - we do I think have to ask ourselves how high a risk is it that children will catch salmonella from playing with an egg-box that's been in my garage for three months...

'We don't let children play with guns - and if they make guns out of something else, we tell them that it's not allowed.'

We don't censor children's play in playwork. If they're playing with guns, it's because they want or need to, so 'gun play' is treated like any other form of play in playwork.

'We don't allow any form of food play in our setting.'

Same as the answer above really. My feeling is that this question comes from the days when people were told that excess food would be sent to Africa where it was needed if it was left to go to waste here. Nowadays we know that nobody in Africa (or anywhere else for that matter) wants carrots sent to them in a parcel - so if children want to play with them, why not?

'What's the matter with children standing in line to have their face painted by an adult?'

While they're standing in line they're probably not playing, and in playwork we're more interested in the children's creativity, so we'd hand the face-paints over!

'Why can't we have whistles to attract children's attention?'

Two reasons - firstly because if they're all playing in the way that we mean play, why would you want their attention? Secondly, because blowing whistles when children are absorbed in their play is not being sensitive to their playful states. The only reason we might possibly need a whistle for is as an emergency signal - and I do mean emergencies, not 'hurry up you're late for tea!'

'If we're not planning activity timetables, how do we make sure that all the religious festivals get celebrated?'

We don't - we can't facilitate play most of the year but at certain times tell the children they're not allowed to do their own thing because we have to 'do a festival.' It's great there are lots of other ways that children learn about different religions and cultures, but playwork doesn't do social or moral education - we just do play!

'One of the ways I help children to play is by lifting them up and giving them aeroplane swings and piggybacks. That's alright, isn't it?'

Nope, sorry! We're not 'one of the kids' when we playwork - we're responsible adults. And as such we need to remember that if we pick up children, we could hurt them as well as ourselves. There are lots of different ways of playing with children - let's leave the physical bits to other adults in their lives.

'We only play co-operative games with the children - this is ok isn't it?'

It would be if the adults are offering co-operative games to the children, rather than making them play co-operative games (sort of defeats the object, doesn't it?!), and if other types of competitive games are not 'banned' competitive by adults. Adults respect children's choices about what they want to play in playwork.

'Isn't it a good idea to split children into groups so they don't play with their best mates all the time?'

From a child's point of view I can see that this would be a very bad idea! Can you imagine - you've been looking forward to messing about with your mate, who's in a different class at school, all day and then some daft adult at the play centre tells you you can't? Adults in playwork respect children's choices about who they play with when.

'You haven't mentioned 'inclusion' once - we're very hot on inclusion!'

Good! All children need play in their lives and playwork is for all children who want or need it. Not all do - and that's ok, there are plenty of other types of provision which can suit children better than a playwork approach or service.

'What about themes and topics?'

Themes and topics belong to activity schemes and activity planning. Playwork follows the child's need to play in whatever direction that goes - we would never try to lead or control that direction by imposing themes or topics.

'I'm not creative - what should I tell the children if they ask me to do something creative with them?'

When we facilitate play, we try to avoid giving answers but instead ask questions and make suggestions to help children to be more creative themselves. We never tell children that we're not creative. If we do, then we're giving them the message that there's a right way and a wrong way to be creative - and that can't be right, it's just fun!

'We always stop for 'tidy up time' - children should learn to clear up after themselves, right?'

Imagine the scene...you've been at a party all night. The company has been good, you've met some really interesting people, had some really good chats, in fact, thoroughly enjoyed yourself...And just as you are preparing to leave, feeling really good and that all is well with the world, your host stops you at the door and says, 'I'm really glad you enjoyed yourself so much, now this way to the kitchen for your washing up stint before you can go home.' How do you feel now - pretty deflated?

And that's just about what it must feel for a child when they're told, 'It's half an hour until home time, now we'll all clear up.' Playwork is about children playing - when we're playworking we're only interested in children playing, not ensuring that they know how to tidy away after themselves - that's a parent's job. Sorry folks, it's the adult's responsibility to clear up in playwork - we'll just have to lump it!

Bibliography / Further Reading

Bonel, P. and Lindon, J. (1996) *Good Practice in Play and Playwork* Stanley Thornes

Davy, A. with Gallagher, J. (2001) *Playwork* Thomson Learning

Else, P. and Sturrock, G. (2003) *The Play Cycle - An Introduction to Psycholudics.* Common Threads Publications Ltd.

Holland, P. (2003) *We don't play with guns here* Open University Press

Hughes, B. (2001) *Evolutionary playwork and reflective analytic practice.* Routledge

Hughes, B. (2002) *A playworker's taxonomy of play types,* 2nd edn. Common Threads Publications Ltd.

Isles-Buck, E. and Newstead, S. (2003) *Essential Skills for Managers of Child-Centred Settings* David Fulton

Making sense - *playwork in practice* (2002) PLAYLINK

National Playing *Fields Association* (2000) Best Play -
What Play Provision Should Do for Children

Nicholson, S. (1971) *How not to cheat children - the
Theory of Loose Parts*, Landscape Architecture

PLAYLINK (2003) *Open for Play*

Playwords - subscription magazine for those working in
children's play - available from Common Threads
Publications Ltd., details below.

Playwork Theory and Practice (2002) ed. Brown, F.
Open University Press

Tassoni, P. (2001) *Playwork* Heinemann

Hughes, B., (2001) *The First Claim.* Cardiff: PlayWales

Waters, P. (2004) Play Clips 1 - *Understanding Play Types*.
(Video/DVD + notes) Common Threads Publications
Ltd.

Further contacts
Common Threads - training and publications for
people working in children's play
T: 07000 785215 E: info@commonthreads.co.uk

SkillsActive - Sector Skills Council for Playwork
T: 0207 6322000 E: info@skillsactive.com